THE OFFICIAL
ENGLAND CRICKET
ANNUAL 2025

WE ARE
ENGLAND
CRICKET

Written by **Andy Greeves**
Designed by **John Anderson**
Contributions by **Cathryn Greeves and Justin Cox**

A Grange Publication

Official licensed product of England and Wales Cricket Board Limited (ECB). Published under licence by Grange Communications Ltd, Edinburgh. The Three Lions and Crown logo, We Are England Cricket logo and England Cricket Merchandise logo are registered trademarks of ECB. Printed in the EU.

Photographs © ECB, Getty and Alamy

ISBN 978-1-915879-82-0

CONTENTS

WELCOME TO THE OFFICIAL
ENGLAND CRICKET
ANNUAL 2025

In this Annual, we profile the players who make up England Men's, Women's, and Disability teams' senior squads as well as Head Coaches, Brendon McCullum and Jon Lewis.

On the back of a busy year in 2024, we review England Men's performances at the ICC T20 World Cup and find out how they fared in their Test series against the West Indies. We also look at England Women's displays in their white-ball series against Pakistan and New Zealand.

There's also a look ahead to the 2025 ICC Champions Trophy and 2025 ICC Women's Cricket World Cup while we catch up with musician and presenter Felix White, who is a huge England cricket fan.

The Annual is brought to life with action photography while there are other features, puzzles, and plenty more besides to entertain England cricket fans of all ages!

COME ON ENGLAND!

WWW.ECB.CO.UK
SHOP.ECB.CO.UK

ENGLAND
WOMEN'S TEAM

PERSONNEL

Coach Jon Lewis
Captain Heather Knight

WOMEN'S TESTS

First Test
v Australia at the Brisbane Exhibition Ground, Brisbane, 28–31 December 1934

Test Record
Played 100, Won 20, Drawn 64, Lost 16

WOMEN'S ONE DAY INTERNATIONALS

First WODI
v International XI at County Cricket Ground, Hove, 23 June 1973

WODI Record
Played 392, Won 231, Lost 146
(2 ties and 13 no result)

Women's Cricket World Cup Best Result
Winners 1973, 1993, 2009 and 2017

WOMEN'S TWENTY20 INTERNATIONAL

First WT20I
v New Zealand at County Cricket Ground, Hove, 5 August 2004

WT20I Record
Played 195, Won 140, Lost 50
(3 ties and 2 no result)

Women's T20 World Cup Best Result
Winners 2009

PLAYER RECORDS

Most Career Women's Test Appearances
Jan Brittin 27 matches (1979-1998)

Most Career Women's Test Runs
Jan Brittin 1,935 runs in 27 matches (1979-1998)

Most Career Women's Test Wickets
Mary Duggan 77 wickets in 17 matches (1949-1963)

(Information correct as of 29 May 2024 up to and including the final WODI v Pakistan)

Jon Lewis
England Women's Head Coach

Jon Lewis passed his first examination as England Women's Head Coach with flying colours as his team completed a WT20I (5-0) and WODI (3-0) series clean sweep during their tour of the West Indies in December 2022. This success came less than a month on from Lewis' appointment as Head Coach, having previously served the ECB as Elite Pace Bowling Coach and Young Lions Head Coach.

Born in Aylesbury, Buckinghamshire on 26 August 1975, Lewis spent the majority of his playing career with Gloucestershire CCC while his one and only Test appearance for England came against Sri Lanka in 2006. He also made 13 ODI appearances. After spending 16 years at the Bristol County Ground, Lewis represented Surrey (2012-13) and then Sussex (2014). After a year as the club's bowling coach, he became Sussex's assistant head coach in 2015 – a role he held prior to joining the ECB in March 2021.

A successful start to life as England Women's Head Coach continued as he guided his team to the semi-finals of the ICC Women's T20 World Cup in 2023 and an Ashes series draw with Australia that same year. In 2024, England Women enjoyed touring success in New Zealand, a series clean sweep against Pakistan (details of which can be found on pages 48 to 53 of this Annual) and victory against New Zealand in the WODI series (details on pages 54-55). At the time of writing (July 2024), England Women are ranked second in both the ICC's WODI and WT20I World Rankings.

Lewis was appointed as head coach of UP Warriorz ahead of the start of the inaugural Indian Women's Premier League in 2023. It is a role he combines with his position with England Women. During his time as Warriorz head coach, he discovered AI technology which he has since brought into his role with England, saying it provides crucial information on opposition teams and helps make marginal selection decisions.

"We are able to run simulated teams versus the simulated opposition to give us an idea about how those teams may match up against each other," Lewis told ESPNCricinfo in May 2024. "I can send multiple different lineups to the company (London-based company, PSi) and they run, I think it's about 250,000 simulations per team that I send with all the different permutations that could happen through the game."

HEATHER
KNIGHT (OBE)

Role: Right-handed batter

DOB: 26 December 1990

POB: Plymouth, Devon

International debut: 1 March 2010 v India (WODI; Mumbai)

Women's captain Heather is part of an exclusive group of only four players at the time of writing to hit centuries in Test, ODI and T20 formats of the game – the others being teammate Tammy Beaumont as well as Men's cricketers Dawid Malan and Jos Buttler. Heather's notable Test batting displays have included 168* off 294 balls against Australia in January 2022 and 157 (338) versus the same opponents in August 2013. As of June 2024, her 3,765 runs put her fourth on England Women's highest run scorers list in WODIs while she is third on the comparable WT20I list with 2,323 runs in 113 matches. Having led England to victory at the 2017 ICC Women's Cricket World Cup, she was awarded with an OBE (Order of the British Empire) in the Queen's 2018 New Year's Honours list.

NAT
SCIVER-BRUNT

Role: Right-arm fast bowler, right-handed batter

DOB: 20 August 1992

POB: Tokyo, Japan

International debut: 1 July 2013 v Pakistan (WODI; Louth)

An impressive all-rounder, Nat scored England Women's fastest one-day international century (120 off 74 balls overall) in the third WODI against West Indies in September 2023. That was her third century of 2023, having managed 111* and 129 in England's 201 in the three-match WODI series victory over Australia in the Ashes. 2024 started in a similar vein as she smashed 124* off 106 balls in the third WODI during the series whitewash against Pakistan. Nat's 169* against Australia in June 2022 is England Women's fifth-best individual batting WODI performance at the time of writing while her 148* that same year against Australia in the ICC Women's World Cup Final was sadly in vain as England went down to a 71-run defeat.

MAIA
BOUCHIER

Role: Right-handed batter

DOB: 5 December 1998

POB: Kensington, London

International debut: 4 September 2021 v New Zealand (WT20I; Hove)

Maia was awarded her first central contract with England Women in December 2023 at the end of a year that saw her make her WODI debut against Sri Lanka at Chester-le-Street. In the third WODI of that series, she came close to her first international century, scoring 95 from 65 deliveries. Her WODI breakthrough came two years on from her England debut in the second WT20I against New Zealand, in which she scored 25 from 24 balls. She played every match for England at the 2022 Commonwealth Games in Birmingham. She was named Player of the Series as England triumphed in a WT20I series in April 2024 in which she scored the most runs (223). Maia hit her maiden international hundred against New Zealand at Visit Worcestershire New Road in June 2024.

SOPHIA DUNKLEY

Role: Right-handed batter; right-arm spin bowler

DOB: 16 July 1998

POB: Lambeth, London

International debut: 12 November 2018 v Bangladesh (WT20I; Gros Islet)

Sophia made history in June 2021, as she made her Test debut against India and in doing so, became the first black woman to play Test cricket for England. That same month, she also put pen-to-paper on her first central contract, replacing Kirstie Gordon on the 17-player list. The London-born allrounder was named in England's squad for the 2022 Women's Cricket World Cup in New Zealand. That same year, she scored her first century in a WODI match with 107 runs during South Africa's tour of England in June and July 2022.

DANNI WYATT-HODGE

Role: Right-handed batter

DOB: 22 April 1991

POB: Stoke-on-Trent, Staffordshire

International debut: 1 March 2010 v India (WODI; Mumbai)

Danni gave a reminder of her importance to England Women's white-ball teams during Pakistan's tour of England in May 2024, as she hit 87 off 48 balls in a Player of the Match display during the third WT20I at Headingley. She also starred in a 37-run victory for an ECB Development XI against Pakistan at Grace Road, with 57 off 34 balls in a 20-over match. A member of England's ICC Women's World Cup-winning class of 2017, Danni will long be remembered for her 129 off 125 balls in the 2022 World up semi-final against South Africa which helped England into the tournament final with a 137-run victory.

TAMMY BEAUMONT (MBE)

Role: Wicketkeeper, right-handed batter

DOB: 11 March 1991

POB: Dover, Kent

International debut: 4 November 2009 v West Indies (WODI; Basseterre)

England Women's Player of the Series in their 2017 ICC Women's World Cup, Tammy has achieved some big things with the bat whilst representing her country. She hit the most runs at the aforementioned tournament, with her 410 including a 148 off 145 balls as she made the highest partnership for any wicket in a Women's World Cup match (275) with Sarah Taylor, in a 68-run victory over South Africa on 5 July 2017. In June 2023, Tammy became the first English female cricketer to hit a double century with 208 off 331 balls against Australia. She broke Betty Snowball's highest Test score record in the process, which had previously stood for 88 years!

WE ARE
**ENGLAND
CRICKET**

BESS
HEATH

Role: Wicketkeeper,
right-handed batter

DOB: 20 August 2001

POB: Chesterfield, Derbyshire

International debut:
14 September 2023
v Sri Lanka (WODI; Leicester)

Bess was awarded her first centralised contract by England Women in December 2023, four months on from her first international call up for the series against Sri Lanka. The wicketkeeper-batter made her WODI debut in the final match of that series as England won by 161 at Grace Road in Leicester. Bess' WT20I debut followed soon after in a 5-wicket defeat to India in Mumbai in December 2023.

AMY
JONES

Role: Wicketkeeper,
right-handed batter

DOB: 13 June 1993

POB: Solihull, West Midlands

International debut:
1 February 2013 v Sri Lanka
(WODI; Mumbai)

Amy enjoyed an excellent 2024. She was named Player of the Series as England triumphed 2-1 in their 3-match WODI series in New Zealand and she top-scored with 190 runs. Her 100th WT20I appearance followed, as she put in a Player of the Match performance in the first WT20I against Pakistan at Edgbaston in May 2024. A regular behind the stumps for England Women for many years, Amy is no stranger to impressive batting displays, such as her 94 off 119 balls in the third WODI against India in Nagpur on 12 April 2018. She has shown her leadership qualities too, stepping in as captain in the absence of Nat Sciver-Brunt for the tour of India in September 2022.

LINSEY
SMITH

Role: Slow left-arm bowler;
left-handed batter

DOB: 10 March 1995

POB: Hillingdon, London

International debut:
12 November 2018 v
Bangladesh (WT20I; Gros Islet)

Linsey took 1/17 from four overs on her international senior debut in against Bangladesh during the 2018 ICC Women's T20 World Cup (then called the ICC Women's World T20). She also played against South Africa - again taking one wicket - en route to England becoming tournament runners-up. Linsey took five wickets in the WT20I series during England's tour of India in 2019 and four in the three WT20Is against Sri Lanka that same year. The following summer, she took 2/22 against the West Indies.

ALICE CAPSEY

Role: Left-handed batter, right-arm medium bowler

DOB: 11 August 2004

POB: Redhill, Surrey

International debut: 23 July 2022 v South Africa (WT20I; Worcester)

Aged 18 at the time, Alice was named Player of the Match as England Women sealed a 2-1 victory over Australia in the third W20I of the Women's Ashes on 8 July 2023. She top-scored in the match with 46 runs off 23 balls. This display followed on from her excellent showing at the Commonwealth Games the previous year where she managed the most runs of any England player – 135 in five matches. Her free-scoring form has continued in recent years, with her 51 runs off 27 balls seeing her named Player of the Match in the first WT20I against Sri Lanka in Hove in August 2023 while she hit 44 off 65 in the first WODI against Pakistan in Derby in May 2024.

DANIELLE GIBSON

Role: Right-handed batter, right-arm medium bowler

DOB: 30 April 2001

POB: Cheltenham, Gloucestershire

International debut: 1 July 2023 v Australia (WT20I; Birmingham)

On the back of her WT20I debut against Australia during the Women's Ashes of 2023, Danielle was awarded her first centralised contract by England Women. She ended up playing all three matches in the aforementioned series and took two wickets. She took another wicket - as well as scoring 21 from 15 deliveries - in the third WT20I against Sri Lanka in Derby in September 2023, while she was also selected for the tour of India in December 2023.

FREYA KEMP

Role: Left-handed batter, right-arm medium bowler

DOB: 21 April 2005

POB: Westminster, London

International debut: 25 July 2022 v South Africa (WT20I; Derby)

Shortly after signing her first central contract with England Women in November 2022, Freya suffered a stress fracture in her back which ruled her out for the tour in the West Indies and the 2023 ICC Women's T20 World Cup. Her long-awaited return to the international scene came in England Women's September 2023 series against Sri Lanka, while she went on the tour of India in December 2023. England Women's leading wicket-taker at the Commonwealth Games in 2022, Freya's first half-century (51*) against India in September 2022 saw her become the youngest woman to make a WT20I 50 for England.

ENGLAND
WOMEN'S TEAM

EMMA
LAMB

Role: Right-handed batter, right-arm medium bowler

DOB: 16 December 1997

POB: Preston, Lancashire

International debut: 1 September 2021 v New Zealand (WT20I; Chelmsford)

Injuries to Maia Bouchier and Charlie Dean saw Emma included in England Women's squad for their WT20I series against New Zealand, with her international debut coming in the first match of that series at the County Ground, Chelmsford on 1 September. Her WODI and Test debuts followed in 2022 against Australia and South Africa respectively. She hit 102 off 97 deliveries in a five-wicket victory in the latter fixture. Emma's form that year was rewarded with her first central England Women's contract.

LAUREN
BELL

Role: Right-arm fast bowler

DOB: 2 January 2001

POB: Swindon, Wiltshire

International debut: 27 June 2022 v South Africa (WTest; Taunton)

Lauren played a significant part in the 2023 Women's Ashes series, playing in the Test match as well as three WT20I and three WODI fixtures. Standing 6ft tall and nicknamed 'The Shard', Lauren is a former footballer, who was in Reading FC's academy until the age of 16. Her gradual switch over to cricket saw her make her Women's County Championship debut for Berkshire at the age of just 14! Up to and including the second WT20I against Pakistan in May 2024, she had played three Test, eight WODI and 14 WT20I matches for England.

KATE
CROSS

Role: Right-arm fast bowler

DOB: 3 October 1991

POB: Manchester

International debut: 24 October 2013 v West Indies (WT20I; Bridgetown)

Full name Kathryn Laura Cross, Kate has been part of the England Women's set-up since 2013, when she made her WT20I debut against the West Indies. Since then, she has played over 50 WODIs and, at the time of writing, eight Tests and 16 WT20I. Daughter of the former West Ham United and Manchester City footballer Roger Cross, Kate was included in England's squads for the ICC Women's T20 World Cup in 2020 and 2023 – reaching the semi-finals on both occasions - and the ICC Women's World Cup in 2022.

LAUREN FILER

Role: Right-handed batter; right-arm medium bowler

DOB: 22 December 2000

POB: Bristol

International debut: 22 June 2023 v Australia (WTest; Nottingham)

Lauren was awarded her first centralised contract by England Women in December 2023. This came on the back of her England debut in the one and only Test of the 2023 Women's Ashes series against Australia at Trent Bridge, in which she took four wickets. The pace bowler has since debuted in white-ball cricket for England, with her WODI bow coming against Sri Lanka in September 2023 while her WT20I debut came against New Zealand in March 2024. She took eight wickets in the aforementioned three-match WODI series against Sri Lanka, which saw her named Player of the Series.

MAHIKA GAUR

Role: Right-handed batter; left-arm medium bowler

DOB: 9 March 2006

POB: Reading, Berkshire

International debut (for England): 9 September 2023 v Sri Lanka (WODI; Chester-le-Street)

Mahika had already played cricket at senior WT20I level for the United Arab Emirates in 2019, when she was just 12 years of age. She switched international allegiance in 2023, when she was named in the England Women's 'A' squad for the WT20I series against Australia 'A', while she was named in England Women's squad for the WODI against Sri Lanka a few months later. And what a debut Mahika made, as she took 3 wickets in the 7-wicket victory at the Riverside Ground in Chester-le-Street. At the end of the year, she was awarded a development contract by the ECB.

ISSY WONG

Role: Right-arm fast bowler

DOB: 15 May 2002

POB: Chelsea, London

International debut: 27 June 2022 v South Africa (WTest; Taunton)

Growing up, Issy was part of a programme called Chance to Shine, which encouraged the participation in competitive cricket in state schools in the UK and set her on the path to her eventual Test debut in June 2022. Away from cricket, Issy is a huge Liverpool fan and loves the Disney production *Cars*. She wore shirt number 95 in her early appearances in the Women's Cricket Super League – the same number as Cars' Lightning McQueen.

CHARLIE
DEAN

Role: Right-handed batter; right-arm spin bowler

DOB: 22 December 2000

POB: Burton-on-Trent, Staffordshire

International debut: 16 September 2021 v New Zealand (WODI; Bristol)

Spin bowler Charlie continues to dazzle for England, having burst on to the scene with 10 wickets in the WODI series against New Zealand in autumn 2021 on her international debut. Her 7 wickets across the WT20I series in New Zealand in April 2024 helped her team to a 4-1 victory. In the first match of that series, she became the fastest bowler to take 50 WODI wickets, in just 26 matches, while she also broke the record for the highest 7th wicket partnership in a WODI with an unbroken 130-run stand.

SOPHIE
ECCLESTONE

Role: Left-arm spin bowler

DOB: 6 May 1999

POB: Chester, Cheshire

International debut: 3 July 2016 v Pakistan (WT20I; Bristol)

A spin-bowler extraordinaire, Sophie Ecclestone became an England Women's record breaker during Pakistan's tour in May 2024. She became the leading wicket-taker for England in WT20Is, with 115 wickets during the second WT20I at the County Ground, Northampton, surpassing the previous record held by Katherine Sciver-Brunt OBE. She then became the fastest female cricketer to achieve 100 wickets (in terms of innings - 63) in WODIs. Ecclestone removed Umm-e-Hani and Nashra Sandhu to reach her 100th WODI wicket. Sophie went on to claim wicket 101 in that match as she also removed Aliya Riaz.

SARAH
GLENN

Role: Right-arm leg-spin bowler, right-handed batter

DOB: 27 August 1999

POB: Derby, Derbyshire

International debut: 9 December 2019 v Pakistan (WODI; Kuala Lumpur)

In recent years, Sarah has regularly featured towards the top of the ICC Women's T20I Bowling Rankings. She took 2/23 in the third WT20I in Sri Lanka in September 2023 while she took the most wickets (8) of the 3-0 WT20I victory over Pakistan in May 2024, which included a personal best 4/12 in the first WT20I at Edgbaston. At the time of writing in June 2024, she is the seventh highest England Women's wicket-taker of all-time in WT20Is with 73 in 60 matches.

ENGLAND
MEN'S TEAM

PERSONNEL

Coach Brendon McCullum
Test Captain Ben Stokes
ODI Captain Jos Buttler
T20I Captain Jos Buttler

TESTS

Test Status Acquired 1877

First International
v Australia at the Melbourne Cricket Ground,
Melbourne, 15-19 March 1877

Test Record Played 1,071, Won 392,
Drawn 355, Lost 324

World Test Championship Best Result
Fourth in 2019-2021 and 2021-2023

ONE DAY INTERNATIONALS

First ODI
v Australia at the Melbourne Cricket Ground,
Melbourne, 5 January 1971

ODI Record
Played 797, Won 400, Lost 357
(9 ties and 31 no result)

Cricket World Cup Best Result Winners 2019

TWENTY20 INTERNATIONAL

First T20I v Australia at the Utilita Bowl,
Southampton, 13 June 2005

T20I Record Played 173, Won 90, Lost 75
(2 ties and 6 no result)

**T20 World Cup Best Result
Winners 2010 and 2022**

PLAYER RECORDS

Most Career Test Appearances
James Anderson 187 matches (2003-to date)

Most Career Test Runs
Alastair Cook 12,472 runs in 161 matches
(2006-2018)

Most Career Test Wickets
James Anderson 700 wickets in 187 matches
(2003-to date)

Information correct as of 15 June 2024 (Up to and including the result of the ICC Men's T20 World Cup match v Namibia)

Brendon McCullum
England Men's Head Coach

During the 2022 season, it was ESPN Cricinfo UK editor Andrew Miller who coined the term 'Bazball' to refer to the style of play adopted by England following the appointment of Brendon McCullum – whose nickname is 'Baz' – as Head Coach.

So, what is 'Bazball'? Ali Martin of *The Guardian* once described the philosophy behind it as to: "play positive red-ball [Test] cricket; to soak up pressure when required but also be brave enough to put it back on opponents at the earliest opportunity; to make taking wickets the sole aim in the field; and to strive chiefly for victory across the five days without considering the draw".

It is interesting to note that McCullum himself dislikes the name 'Bazball'. "I don't really like that silly term… I don't have any idea what 'Bazball' is," he once said. "It's not just all crash and burn."

Whether 'Bazball' is a thing or not, the impact McCullum has had on England's play since his appointment as Head Coach back in May 2022 is undeniable. Within the first year of his tenure, England averaged a run rate of 4.65 per over - significantly higher than the next highest in Test match history. England completed the highest Test run rate in a completed innings in international Test history on 1 December 2022, achieving 6.50 per over against Pakistan. At the time of writing, five of the top 10 highest run rates in Test history have all been achieved by McCullum's England.

Such a front-foot approach to cricket is hardly surprising from a man renowned for the speed in which he achieved runs during his playing career. Playing for his native New Zealand, McCullum broke the world record for the fastest Test century as he took just 54 balls to reach 100 on day one of the second Test against Australia in Christchurch on 20 February 2016. Two years earlier, he had become the first New Zealander to score 1,000 test runs in a calendar year,

which included a triple-hundred (302) against India. In his last match before his international retirement, he signed off in true Baz style, hitting 170 against Australia in the second Test, on the day he broke the record for most sixes (107) hit in Test matches.

McCullum retired from all forms of cricket in 2019 when he was appointed as Head Coach of both Trinbago Knight Riders and Kolkata Knight Riders. Three years later he took the top job with England, and just two months into the role his side completed a record chase of 378 to beat India in the fifth Test at Edgbaston in July 2022.

ENGLAND
MEN'S TEAM

WE ARE
ENGLAND
CRICKET

BEN
STOKES

Role: Left-handed batter, right-arm fast medium bowler, Test captain

DOB: 4 June 1991

POB: Christchurch, New Zealand

International debut: 25 August 2011 v Ireland (ODI; Dublin)

Ben won Player of the Match and batted in the dramatic super over as England triumphed in the 2019 ICC Cricket World Cup Final. He top-scored in the 2022 ICC T20 World Cup Final and hit the winning run with six balls to spare as England beat Pakistan in Melbourne. Named the Wisden Leading Cricketer in the World in 2019, 2020 and 2022, Ben retired from ODI cricket in 2022 but continues to lead the way in Test cricket. In the first Test against New Zealand in February 2023, Ben surpassed England Head Coach Brendon McCullum's record of 107 sixes to become the highest six-hitter in Test cricket history.

JOS
BUTTLER

Role: Right-handed batter; wicketkeeper, white-ball captain

DOB: 8 September 1990

POB: Taunton, Somerset

International debut: 31 August 2011 v India (T20I; Manchester)

England's ever-reliable white-ball captain, Jos scored the most runs for England at the 2024 ICC Men's T20 World Cup, hitting 214 across his four matches which included an 83* against the United States at the Kensington Oval. He also made seven dismissals in eight matches at the tournament which he warmed up for by becoming the first England player to reach the 3,000-run mark in T20I cricket in the second T20I against West Indies. England's most capped T20I player, Jos was vice-captain of England's 2019 ICC World Cup-winning team and skipper of the victorious 2022 ICC T20I World Cup team.

HARRY
BROOK

Role: Right-handed batter; right-arm medium bowler

DOB: 22 February 1999

POB: Keighley, West Yorkshire

International debut: 26 January 2022 v West Indies (T20I; Barbados)

Debuting for England in 2022, Harry made an incredible start to his Test career as he amassed 809 runs in his first six appearances. This included scores of 153, 108 and 111 respectively during England's tour of Pakistan in 2022-23 while he scored 75 to help England win the third Test match against Australia during the 2023 Ashes Series. In that innings, he became the fastest batter (by balls faced) to 1,000 runs in Test cricket history. His fine form continued at the 2024 ICC Men's T20 World Cup, as he hit 145 runs, which included 47* off 20 balls in a Player of the Match display against Namibia. He made the joint-second highest number of catches (7) at the tournament along with Glenn Maxwell (Australia) and Tristan Stubbs (South Africa).

ZAK
CRAWLEY

Role: Right-handed batter

DOB: 3 February 1998

POB: Bromley, London

International debut:
29 November 2019 v New Zealand (Test; Hamilton)

Along with Dom Sibley, Zak was one of two England players named in the Wisden Cricketers of the Year in 2021. It came on the back of a memorable 2020 when he scored 267 off 393 balls in the third Test against Pakistan in Southampton. He drew praise from Sir Viv Richards having achieved his second Test century during the first Test against West Indies in Antigua in March 2022 while he became the first England player to score a Test century before lunch on the first day of a Test against Pakistan later that year. More recently, he was England's top-scorer during the 2023-24 tour of India with 407 runs.

BEN
DUCKETT

Role: Left-handed batter; wicketkeeper

DOB: 17 October 1994

POB: Farnborough, London

International debut:
7 October 2016 v Bangladesh (ODI; Mirpur)

The highlight of Ben's England career to date came against Pakistan in December 2022 when he scored his maiden Test century and achieved the fastest double-century partnership in Test cricket history off 233 balls along with Zak Crawley. He scored an impressive first innings 153 off 151 balls during the third Test against India in Rajkot in February 2024 but could not prevent his side going down to their second largest-ever Test defeat. Ben was included in England's squad for the ICC T20 World Cup later that year.

SHOAIB
BASHIR

Role: Right-arm off-break bowler; right-handed batter

DOB: 13 October 2003

POB: Chertsey, Surrey

International debut:
2 February 2024 v India (Test; Visakhapatnam)

In only his second Test appearance, Shoaib claimed his maiden Test five-wicket haul, finishing first innings of the fourth Test against India in February with 5/119. He also managed a five-wicket haul in the fifth and final Test in Dharamshala and against the West Indies in the second innings of the second Test at Trent Bridge in July 2024. Aged 20 years and 282 days at the time, he became the youngest England spinner to take a five-wicket haul on home soil in the process.

OLLIE
POPE

Role: Right-handed batter, Test vice-captain

DOB: 2 January 1998

POB: Chelsea, London

International debut: 9 August 2018 v India (Test; Lord's)

In the five-match Test tour of India in 2024, Ollie played a match-winning knock of 196 runs in the second innings of the first match – the fourth highest score achieved by an Englishman in India. This came on the back of a mixed 2023, when he was appointed as England's Test vice-captain and achieved the fastest Test double-hundred off just 207 balls against Ireland at Lord's but suffered a dislocated shoulder against Australia that saw him ruled out of action for several months.

JOE
ROOT

Role: Right-handed batter; right-arm spin bowler

DOB: 30 December 1990

POB: Sheffield, South Yorkshire

International debut: 13 December 2012 v India (Test; Nagpur)

Joe was the highest run-scorer among all active batsmen at the time of writing when he was closing in on Mahela Jayawardene's tally of 11,814 runs during his Sri Lanka career between 1997 and 2014. When Joe surpasses that number, he will move to ninth on the list of the highest run-scorers of all time in Test cricket. Awarded an MBE in the 2020 New Year Honours list for his services to cricket, Joe was the ICC Men's Test Cricketer of the Year in 2021 while he has been named in the ICC Test Team of the Year on five occasions. During his tenure as England's Test team captain between February 2017 and April 2022, Joe skippered in more Test matches (64) than any other player and also oversaw most Test victories, with 27.

REHAN
AHMED

Role: Right-handed batter, right-arm leg-spin bowler

DOB: 13 August 2004

POB: Nottingham, Nottinghamshire

International debut: 17 December 2022 v Pakistan (Test; Karachi)

Aged just 18 years and 205 days old at the time, Rehan became the youngest player to represent England across all formats when he made his ODI debut in the final match of the three-match series against Bangladesh in March 2023. He also holds the record for England's youngest Test player at 18 years and 126 days, achieved against Pakistan in December 2022 – an occasion he marked with a five-wicket haul in the third and final match of the series in Karachi. The 2022 BBC Young Sports Personality of the Year nominee took 11 wickets and scored 76 runs in three Test matches at the start of 2024.

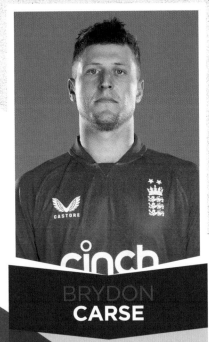

BRYDON CARSE

Role: Right-handed batter, right-arm fast bowler

DOB: 31 July 1995

POB: Cape Town, South Africa

International debut: 8 July 2021 v Pakistan (ODI; Cardiff)

Brydon was one of five England players to make their debut in the 9-wicket victory over Pakistan at Sophia Gardens in July 2021. In the third match of that series, he took his maiden five-wicket haul in ODIs. Renowned for his pace bowling, one of Brydon's deliveries clocked 91mph in the second ODI against the Netherlands in May 2022 while he made an impressive T20I debut, taking 3/23 in the first T20I against New Zealand as he won Player of the Match in a 7-wicket victory for England in August 2023.

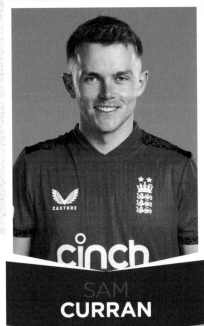

SAM CURRAN

Role: Left-arm fast bowler; left-handed batter

DOB: 3 June 1998

POB: Northampton, Northamptonshire

International debut: 1 June 2018 v Pakistan (Test; Leeds)

Sam is from a cricketing family with his grandfather, father and brothers Tom and Ben all having had professional careers in the sport. The Northamptonshire-born all-rounder was Player of the Tournament at the 2022 ICC T20 World Cup as he took 13 wickets in England's triumphant campaign. In the opening match of that tournament, he became the first England player to take a 5-wicket haul in T20Is, as his 5/10 earned him the Player of the Match award. After his World Cup heroics, Sam was awarded with an MBE in the 2023 Birthday Honours for his services to cricket.

LIAM LIVINGSTONE

Role: Right-handed batter; right-arm leg break/off break bowler

DOB: 4 August 1993

POB: Barrow-in-Furness, Cumbria

International debut: 23 June 2017 v South Africa (ODI; Taunton)

Awarded the Most Valuable Player in the inaugural The Hundred back in 2021, Liam became just the third England player to score a century in a T20I match with 103 runs against Pakistan that same year. In 2022, he scored 50 off 17 balls as England scored 498/4 against Netherlands – the highest ODI score in the history of cricket – while he was also a member of the England team that won the ICC T20 World Cup that year. He warmed up for his appearance at the 2024 ICC T20 World Cup by taking three wickets in the 2-0 T20I series victory over Pakistan in May.

CHRIS
WOAKES

Role: Right-arm fast bowler; right-handed batter

DOB: 2 March 1989

POB: Birmingham

International debut: 12 January 2011 v Australia (T20I; Adelaide)

Chris won the Compton-Miller Medal as England's Player of the Series in the 2023 Ashes as he picked up 19 wickets across 6 innings. He is one of six players to feature in England's successes at both the 2019 ICC Cricket World Cup and 2022 ICC T20I World Cup. Chris took three wickets in the semi-final victory over Australia in the 2019 competition, as he featured in every tournament match. He was ever-present in England's 2022 T20I tournament too.

JONNY
BAIRSTOW

Role: Right-handed batter; wicketkeeper

DOB: 26 September 1989

POB: Bradford, West Yorkshire

International debut: 16 September 2011 v India (ODI; Cardiff)

Jonny joined an elite group of just 17 English players to have made 100-plus Test appearances when he brought his century up in the final Test against India in Dharamshala in March 2024. During the same series, he also surpassed the 6,000-run tally in Test cricket. A former youth footballer with Leeds United, Jonny was also named Young Wisden Schools Cricketer of the Year back in 2007. Along with Ben Stokes, he holds the record for the highest sixth-wicket stand in Test cricket – a staggering 399, which came against South Africa during England's 2015-16 tour.

JAMIE
SMITH

Role: Right-handed batter; wicketkeeper

DOB: 2 July 2000

POB: Epsom, Surrey

International debut: 23 September 2023 v Ireland (ODI; Nottingham)

Jamie burst onto the Test scene in the summer of 2024. Along with Gus Atkinson and Mikyle Louis, he made his red-ball debut in the first Test of West Indies tour of England at Lord's in July 2024 and scored 70 in his first innings. His first Test century arrived a month later as he hit 111 off 148 against Sri Lanka at Old Trafford. That saw him become only the third England player, after Harry Brook and Bryan Valentine, to score more than 70 in three of their first five Test innings.

JOFRA ARCHER

Role: Right-arm fast bowler

DOB: 1 April 1995

POB: Bridgetown, Barbados

International debut: 3 May 2019 (ODI, Malahide)

Jofra made a welcome return to the England fold during Pakistan's tour in May 2024. He took two wickets in his comeback game in the first T20I at Edgbaston in a 23-run victory, after missing over a year of action due to an elbow injury. The fast bowler burst onto the international scene back in 2019 when he bowled England's successful super over in the ICC Cricket World Cup Final victory over New Zealand. Unsurprisingly, he was included in the Team of the Tournament while he was also named as one of the five Widen Cricketers of the Year in 2020.

GUS ATKINSON

Role: Right-arm fast bowler

DOB: 19 January 1998

POB: Chelsea, London

International debut: 1 September 2023 v New Zealand (T20I, Manchester)

Gus fully justified his maiden international call up as he took 4/20 in the 95-run victory over New Zealand in the second T20I at Old Trafford in September 2023 – the best figures of any debutant England men's bowler. He took the notable wicket of Babar Azam against Pakistan at the 2023 ICC Cricket World Cup, while his first Test against West Indies in July 2024 saw him take a 7-wicket haul. His 7/45 was the second-best bowling figures on a Test debut by an English cricketer.

MATTY POTTS

Role: Right-arm fast medium bowler

DOB: 29 October 1998

POB: Sunderland, Tyne and Wear

International debut: 2 June 2022 v New Zealand (Test, Lord's)

Matty marked his England debut with figures of 4/13 in the first innings of the first Test against New Zealand at Lord's in June 2022 and followed up with 3/55 in the second innings. He had featured in six Test matches at the time of writing, with his most recent coming against Ireland in June 2023. He has also featured in a number of ODI matches, with his international baptism in white-ball cricket coming against South Africa at Chester-le-Street a month after his Test debut.

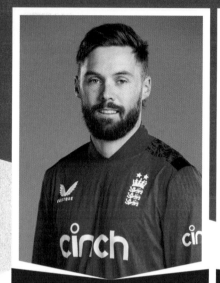

PHIL
SALT

Role: Right-handed batter; wicketkeeper

DOB: 28 August 1996

POB: Bodelwyddan, Wales

International debut: 8 July 2021 v Pakistan (ODI; Cardiff)

Fittingly for a Welshman, Phil made his England debut in the first ODI against Pakistan in July 2021 at Sophia Gardens in Cardiff. His T20I bow came against the West Indies in Barbados in January 2022 meanwhile. The wicketkeeper-batter has achieved centuries in both white-ball formats, hitting a ODI 122 against the Netherlands in June 2022 while he managed a score of 119 in a T20I during England's 2023-24 tour of the West Indies. He was part of England's victorious squad at the 2022 ICC Men's T20 World Cup and while he was in the 15-man travelling party for the 2024 tournament, where he smashed an unbeaten 87 off 47 against the West Indies.

JOSH
TONGUE

Role: Right-arm fast bowler; right-handed batter

DOB: 15 November 1997

POB: Redditch, Worcestershire

International debut: 1 June 2023 v Ireland (Test; Lord's)

Josh made his Test debut against Ireland in June 2023 and took 5/66 in the second innings. The fast-bowler featured in the second Test against Australia on 28 June-2 July 2023 and duly took 3/98 in the first innings at Lord's. In 2024, Josh and Worcestershire teammate Dillon Pennington moved to Nottinghamshire with Josh putting pen-to-paper on a three-year contract.

REECE
TOPLEY

Role: Left-arm fast-medium bowler; right-handed batter

DOB: 21 February 1994

POB: Ipswich, Suffolk

International debut: 31 August 2015 v Australia (T20I; Cardiff)

A member of England's squad for the 2023 ICC Cricket World Cup and 2024 ICC T20 World Cup, Reece made both his ODI and T20I debuts during Australia's tour of England back in 2015. He made history in July 2022 by achieving the best figures for an English bowler in ODI cricket as he took 6/24 in the second ODI against India at Lord's. Yet to make his Test debut at the time of writing, Reece is the son of former Essex and Surrey cricketer Don Topley while his uncle, Peter Topley was also a first-class cricketer.

MARK
WOOD

Role: Right-arm fast bowler

DOB: 11 January 1990

POB: Ashington, Northumberland

International debut: 8 May 2015 v Ireland (ODI; Dublin)

Mark was a key member of the England team that won the 2019 ICC World Cup and 2022 ICC T20I World Cup. His 18 wickets at the 2019 ICC World Cup came at a strike-rate of 29.8 while he played in every Super 12 game at the 2022 ICC T20I World Cup, and was the fastest bowler at the tournament, before missing out the semi-final and final due to injury. Mark was named Man of the Match as he took a collective 7-100 and scored 40 runs from 16 balls during the 2023 Ashes series.

JACK
LEACH

Role: Left-arm spin bowler

DOB: 22 June 1991

POB: Taunton, Somerset

International debut: 30 March 2018 v New Zealand (Test; Christchurch)

Google 'Jack Leach' and you'll quickly be reminded of his famous one not out in his last-wicket partnership with Ben Stokes as England beat Australia by one wicket in the third Ashes Test back in 2019. Since that great Headingley moment, Jack has shown himself to be more than a one-hit wonder. He took 25 wickets across five Tests against Pakistan and New Zealand in the winter of 2022-23 before injury sadly ruled him out for the 2023 Ashes. He also missed the last three Tests of the tour of India in 2024 with a problem with his left knee that ultimately required surgery.

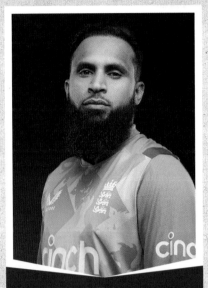

ADIL
RASHID

Role: Right-arm leg-spin bowler

DOB: 17 February 1988

POB: Bradford, West Yorkshire

International debut: 5 June 2009 v Netherlands (T20I; Lord's)

Along with Chris Jordan (10/83) and Jofra Archer (10/158), Adil took 10-wickets (10/168) at the 2024 ICC Men's T20 World Cup, making him England's joint-top wicket-taker at the tournament. He was Player of the Match in the 8-wicket victory over Oman as he took four wickets off 11 balls and in the Super 8 encounter with the United States. Awarded an MBE in 2023, the right-arm leg break bowler is England's highest wicket-taker among spin bowlers in both ODIs and T20Is and the country's second-highest wicket-taker in T20Is overall behind Chris Jordan.

ENGLAND
DISABILITY TEAMS

ENGLAND CRICKET

Deaf Cricket Team

Deaf cricket has been played for over 50 years in England while the England Deaf Cricket Team has been participating in international matches since 1992. Since then, they have twice been Deaf Cricket World Cup runners-up in 1995/6 and 2005.

Currently captained by George Greenway - the runner-up in the 2023 Deaf Sports Personality of the Year award - England Men's Deaf Team hosted a pulsating IT20 series against India during the summer of 2024, that sadly ended in a 5-2 series defeat for the home team.

The England Deaf Cricket Team has a mixture of BSL users, Sign-Supported English users and spoken English. Internationally, deaf cricketers must have a minimum hearing loss of 55dB in the better ear. At the grassroots - county and regional level - the entry requirement is that you can show you are deaf or hard of hearing. More information can be found at:
www.englanddeafcricket.co.uk

The England Deaf Cricket Team is one of four England disability teams that compete at home and abroad – the others being for those with a Physical Disability (PD), Learning Disability (LD) or Visual Impairment (VI). England VI will play an Ashes series to take place in Australia in November 2024 whilst the Physical Disability are preparing for a World Cup in India early 2025, while the PD and LD sides face various county and select XI sides.

Big news from the England PD team in the summer of 2024 was the appointment of Chris Highton as Head Coach and Lloyd Tennant as Assistant Head Coach on two-year contracts.

In addition to the Men's Teams, England also has a Women's Pan-disability training squad and a Visually Impaired squad.

For fixture information and the latest news on England's disability teams visit
www.ecb.co.uk/england/disability

Physical Disability Team

Learning Disability Team

Visually Impaired Team

27

GEORGE **GREENWAY**

DOB: 11 March 1993

International debut:
18 January 2011 v Australia
(Geelong)

Favourite Player:
Pat Cummins & Ben Stokes

STEPHEN **GEORGE**

DOB: 9 August 1984

International debut:
26 January 2004 v Australia
(Sydney)

Favourite Player:
Jonty Rhodes

UMESH **VALJEE** (MBE)

DOB: 30 September 1969

International debut:
6 January 1992 v Australia
(Perth)

Favourite Player:
Virat Kohli

JAMES **SCHOFIELD**

DOB: 18 June 1986

International debut:
18 January 2011 v Australia
(Geelong)

Favourite Player: Trent Boult,
Mark Wood, Meg Lanning,
Ellyse Perry, Nat Sciver-Brunt

JOSH **PRICE**

DOB: 20 October 1990

International debut:
8 June 2022 v Australia
(Brisbane)

Favourite Player:
Moeen Ali

JAKE **OAKES**

DOB: 10 May 1995

International debut:
27 June 2015 v Denmark
(Denmark)

Favourite Player:
David Wiese, Kate Cross &
Umesh Valjee MBE

CAMERON **SWEENEY**

DOB: 21 December 1997

International debut:
18 June 2024 v India (Derby)

Favourite Player:
Ben Stokes & Mark Wood

JOEL **HARRIS**

DOB: 6 August 1994

International debut:
4 September 2013 v South
Africa (Pretoria)

Favourite Player:
Andrew Flintoff

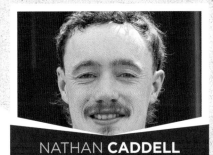

NATHAN **CADDELL**

DOB: 22 June 1996

International debut: 8 June 2022 v Australia (Brisbane)

Favourite Player: Andrew Flintoff

MATT **BAILEY**

DOB: 29 June 2000

International debut: 16 June 2022 v Australia (Brisbane)

Favourite Player: Andrew Flintoff & James Anderson

JAMES **O'CONNOR**

DOB: 27 August 1996

International debut: Yet to make international debut

Favourite Player: Shane Warne

JAMES **DIXON**

DOB: 15 November 1986

International debut: 22 November 2005 v South Africa (Lucknow, India)

Favourite Player: Bob Willis & James Anderson

HENRY **WAINMAN**

DOB: 18 August 1994

International debut: 28 August 2013 v South Africa (Pretoria)

Favourite Player: Andrew Flintoff

MOHAMMED **FAROOQ**

DOB: 10 January 1980

International debut: 20 November 2005 v Nepal (Lucknow, India)

Favourite Player: Stuart Broad & Glenn McGrath

LUKE **RILEY**

DOB: 19 December 2001

International debut: 27 June 2024 v India (Leicester)

Favourite Player: Harry Brook

ENGLAND
ENGLAND PHYSICAL DISABILITY
(PD) TEAM

WE ARE
**ENGLAND
CRICKET**

CALLUM **FLYNN**

DOB: 12 March 1995

International debut:
11 February 2012 v Pakistan
(Dubai)

Favourite Player:
Andrew Flintoff

ALEX **HAMMOND**

DOB: 29 March 1995

International debut:
21 March 2014 v Pakistan
(Dubai)

Favourite Player:
Sachin Tendulkar

ANGUS **BROWN**

DOB: 28 July 2002

International debut:
5 August 2019 v Pakistan
(Kidderminster)

Favourite Player: Joe Root

ANTHONY **CLAPHAM**

DOB: 21 March 1990

International debut:
28 January 2024 v India
(Ahmedabad)

Favourite Player:
Kevin Pietersen

BEN **SUTTON**

DOB: 11 November 2002

International debut:
5 August 2019 v Pakistan
(Kidderminster)

Favourite Player:
Moeen Ali

BRENDON **PARR**

DOB: 27 June 1992

International debut:
28 January 2024 v India
(Ahmedabad)

Favourite Player:
Jos Buttler

CAMERON **COOPER**

DOB: 3 August 2001

International debut:
Yet to make international debut

Favourite Player:
Mark Wood

DANIEL **REYNALDO**

DOB: 2 May 1995

International debut:
14 February 2012 v Pakistan
(Dubai)

Favourite Player:
Shane Warne

FRED **BRIDGES**

DOB: 13 December 1990

International debut:
11 February 2012 v Pakistan
(Dubai)

Favourite Player:
Graham Thorpe

HUGO **HAMMOND**

DOB: 20 November 1996

International debut:
4 September 2015 v
Bangladesh (Dhaka)

Favourite Player:
Alex Hammond

JAMES **NORDIN**

DOB: 6 April 2000

International debut:
6 February 2024 v India
(Ahmedabad)

Favourite Player:
Will Flynn

JAMIE **GOODWIN**

DOB: 5 July 1993

International debut:
4 September 2015 v
Bangladesh (Dhaka)

Favourite Player:
Andrew Flintoff

JORDAN **WILLIAMS**

DOB: 6 July 1992

International debut:
21 March 2014 v Pakistan
(Dubai)

Favourite Player:
Andrew Flintoff

LIAM **O'BRIEN**

DOB: 26 March 1999

International debut:
8 July 2018 v Pakistan
(Barnards Green)

Favourite Player:
Andrew Flintoff

LIAM **THOMAS**

DOB: 7 February 1994

International debut:
11 February 2012 v Pakistan
(Dubai)

Favourite Player:
Jos Buttler

SAMUEL **KUMAR**

DOB: 30 May 2003

International debut:
28 January 2024 v India
(Ahmedabad)

Favourite Player:
Shane Warne

WILLIAM **FLYNN**

DOB: 4 April 2000

International debut:
8 July 2018 v Pakistan
(Barnards Green)

Favourite Player:
Ian Bell

ENGLAND
ENGLAND LEARNING DISABILITY
(LD) TEAM

WE ARE
**ENGLAND
CRICKET**

CHRIS **EDWARDS**

DOB: 2 March 1993

International debut:
4 Dec 2009 v Australia
(Melbourne)

Favourite Player:
Chris Woakes

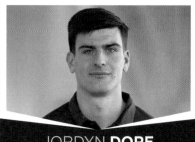

JORDYN **DORE**

DOB: 22 August 2000

International debut:
11 October 2019 v Australia
(Brisbane)

Favourite Player:
Stuart Broad

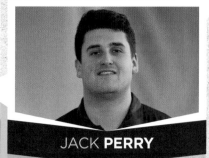

JACK **PERRY**

DOB: 26 January 2000

International debut:
10 July 2017 v South Africa
(Chester)

Favourite Player:
Marnus Labuschagne

ANDREW **MOWATT**

DOB: 12 January 1994

International debut:
11 October 2019 v Australia
(Brisbane)

Favourite Player:
Ian Botham

DAN **LEVEY**

DOB: 23 November 1994

International debut:
17 November 2011 v Australia
(Kimberley)

Favourite Player:
Chris Gayle

ALFIE **PYLE**

DOB: 28 July 2002

International debut:
12 November 2023 v Australia
(Pretoria)

Favourite Player:
Chris Edwards

ALEX **JERVIS**

DOB: 19 June 1995

International debut:
17 March 2015 v Australia
(Doncaster, Australia)

Favourite Player:
Joe Root

JON **GALE**

DOB: 21 July 1994

International debut:
16 November 2011 v South
Africa (Kimberley)

Favourite Player:
Ian Bell

MARTIN **HENDERSON**

DOB: 25 July 1987

International debut:
11 October 2019 v Australia
(Brisbane)

Favourite Player:
Mark Wood

ENGLAND
ENGLAND LEARNING DISABILITY
(LD) TEAM

KESTER **SAINSBURY**

DOB: 5 April 2003

International debut:
8 October 2019 v Australia
(Brisbane)

Favourite Player:
Malcolm Marshall

TOM **WILSON**

DOB: 30 June 1993

International debut:
14 July 2017 v Australia
(Tattenhall)

Favourite Player:
Jonathan Trott

JAIDEV **CHARAN**

DOB: 28 November 1998

International debut:
18 November 2023 v South
Africa (Pretoria)

Favourite Player:
Jonny Bairstow

BEN **MASON**

DOB: 23 June 2004

International debut:
14 November 2023 v South
Africa (Pretoria)

Favourite Player:
Roelof van der Merwe

KIERON **MCKINNEY**

DOB: 16 October 1982

International debut:
9 October 2019 v Australia
(Brisbane)

Favourite Player:
Brian Lara

TAYLER **YOUNG**

DOB: 16 May 1995

International debut:
16 November 2011 v South
Africa (Kimberley)

Favourite Player:
Ben Stokes

RONNIE **JACKSON**

DOB: 9 February 1999

International debut:
17 March 2015 v Australia
(Doncaster, Australia)

Favourite Player:
Andrew Flintoff

BOB **HEWITT**

DOB: 5 June 1994

International debut:
17 March 2015 v Australia
(Doncaster, Australia)

Favourite Player:
Adil Rashid

DAN **BOWSER**

DOB: 11 March 1998

International debut:
17 March 2015 v Australia
(Doncaster, Australia)

Favourite Player:
Joe Root

33

ENGLAND
BLIND AND VISUALLY IMPAIRED
(VI) TEAM

MATTHEW **DEAN**

DOB: 16 March 1983

International debut:
22 August 2004 v Australia
(Bradfield)

Favourite Player:
David Gower

EDWARD **HOSSELL**

DOB: 2 June 1993

International debut:
27 November 2014 v South
Africa (Cape Town)

Favourite Player:
Andrew Flintoff

NATHAN **FOY**

DOB: 17 June 1980

International debut:
19 November 2002 v Pakistan
(Bradfield)

Favourite Player:
Heindrich Swanepoel

LUKE **SUGG**

DOB: 27 September 1989

International debut:
22 August 2004 v Australia
(Bradfield)

Favourite Player:
Jos Buttler

MATTHEW **PAGE**

DOB: 3 December 1990

International debut:
6 December 2012 v South
Africa (Bangalore)

Favourite Player:
Heindrich Swanepoel

NATHAN **JAMIESON**

DOB: 30 April 1993

International debut:
12 November 2019 v Pakistan
(Ajman, UAE)

Favourite Player:
Kevin Pietersen

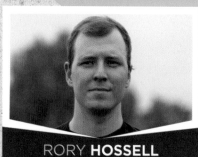

RORY **HOSSELL**

DOB: 22 September 1997

International debut:
31 January 2017 v Pakistan
(Delhi)

Favourite Player:
Mark Wood

DAVID **HOWELLS**

DOB: 8 August 2003

International debut:
20 August 2023 v Australia
(Birmingham)

Favourite Player:
Sam Curran

GARETH **JONES**

DOB: 9 January 1984

International debut:
4 October 2018 v India
(Bangalore)

Favourite Player:
Graham Gooch

MARK **TURNHAM**

DOB: 22 June 1976

International debut:
10 December 2006 v New Zealand (Islamabad)

Favourite Player:
Sachin Tendulkar

MAHOMED-ABRAAR **KHATRI**

DOB: 8 November 1990

International debut:
22 August 2007 v India (Redditch)

Favourite Player:
Andrew Flintoff

SAMUEL **HOSKIN**

DOB: 23 July 1999

International debut:
20 August 2023 v Australia (Birmingham)

Favourite Player:
Jos Buttler

MOSHFIQUE **AHMED**

DOB: 31 January 1982

International debut:
24 August 2023 v Pakistan (Birmingham)

Favourite Player:
Ben Stokes

JUSTIN **HOLLINGSWORTH**

DOB: 1 January 1997

International debut:
5 December 2012 v Sri Lanka (Bangalore)

Favourite Player:
Stuart Broad

ANDREW **POWERS**

DOB: 27 October 1985

International debut:
30 January 2006 v Sri Lanka (Melbourne)

Favourite Player:
Andrew Flintoff

WE ARE
ENGLAND
CRICKET

ENGLAND
BLIND AND VISUALLY IMPAIRED
(VI) TEAM

CHARLTON DAVIS

DOB: 5 September 2001

Favourite player:
Zak Crawley

CHRIS STYLES

DOB: 1 May 1998

Favourite player:
Jos Buttler

GERALD PORTER

DOB: 1 February 1978

Favourite player:
AB de Villiers

MO GHALIB

DOB: 1 October 1984

Favourite player:
Moeen Ali / Jos Buttler

SHAKIR IQBAL

DOB: 7 March 1992

Favourite player:
Shahid Afridi

TOKEER AKHTAR

DOB: 29 March 1987

Favourite player:
Imran Khan

CHAMPIONS TROPHY

Preview

AFTER AN EIGHT-YEAR HIATUS, THE ICC CHAMPIONS TROPHY RETURNS IN 2025.

HISTORY

Created by the International Cricket Council (ICC), the ICC Champions Trophy was first staged in Bangladesh in 1998. The top eight ranked teams in the preceding edition of the Cricket World Cup (including the hosts of the Champions Trophy) secure a berth for the tournament, with 13 different nations to date having taken part in the One Day International (ODI) format competition.

Known as the ICC KnockOut Trophy for the first two editions in 1998 and 2000, it was South Africa who were the competition's first victors, as they secured a 4-wicket victory over West Indies in the final of 1 November 1998. New Zealand beat India in the final of the 2000 tournament meanwhile, which was staged in Kenya.

India and Sri Lanka had to share the trophy in 2002 as both their final of 29 September 2002 and rescheduled final a day later couldn't be completed due to heavy rain in Colombo, Sri Lanka.

England hosted the tournament for the first time in 2004 and reached their inaugural final. The Three Lions' Marcus Trescothick managed the most runs of the tournament (261) while teammate Andrew Flintoff (9) took the most wickets. But it was an Ian Bradshaw-inspired Sri Lanka who took the spoils in the final, staged at The Oval on 25 September 2004, winning by two wickets.

Australia were victorious in the next two tournaments, staged in India in 2006 and in South Africa in 2009. England (and Wales) had the honour of hosting the 2013 edition and once again progressed to the final on home soil. India achieved a 5-run victory over the hosts at Edgbaston on 23 June 2023. In the process, MS Dhoni became the first captain to win ICC T20 World Cup (2007), Cricket World Cup (2011) and ICC Champions Trophy.

England and Wales also hosted the most recent tournament in 2017, which was won by Pakistan. The 2021 Champions Trophy, scheduled to be held in India, was instead converted into a World T20 meet.

2025 TOURNAMENT

Hosts Pakistan will compete in the 2025 ICC Championship trophy alongside the seven other best performing nations at the 2023 Cricket World Cup - Afghanistan, Australia, Bangladesh, England, India, New Zealand and South Africa. Of those teams, Afghanistan will be making their tournament debut.

The eight teams will compete in two groups of four, with the top two nations from each group progressing to the semi-finals. At the time of writing, the groups and match schedule was yet to be announced. Three cities - Karachi, Lahore and Rawalpindi – will host the games with India scheduled to play the entire tournament in Lahore. The first match will take place on 19 February 2025 while the final will be played on 9 March 2025.

CROSS WORD

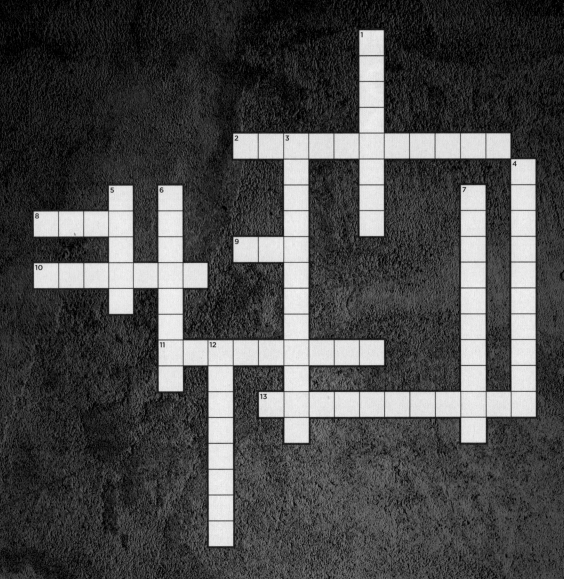

ACROSS

2. Tammy Beaumont smashed 119 off 107 balls in the third WODI against this touring nation in July 2022 (5,6)

8. England's first win at the 2024 ICC Men's T20 World Cup came against this nation (4)

9. Host nation of the 2024 ICC Women's T20 World Cup (1,1,1)

10. England beat this African nation by 41 runs (DLS method) in Group B of the 2024 ICC Men's T20 World Cup (7)

11. This nation famously provides England's opponents for The Ashes (9)

13. Ben Stokes hit his first ICC Cricket World Cup century against this European nation in 2023 (11)

DOWN

1. Nat Sciver-Brunt scored England Women's fastest one-day international century (120 off 74 balls overall) in the third WODI ag (3,5)

3. They hosted the 2024 ICC Men's T20 World Cup along with the West Indies (6,6)

4. James Anderson took his best Test figures of 7-42 and also claimed his 500th Test wicket against this touring nation in 2017 (4,6)

5. Tom Hartley's incredible seven-wicket haul on his Test debut came against this team (5)

6. England Women achieved a series clean sweep against this touring nation in May 2024 (8)

7. The Women's team of this southern hemisphere nation toured England in June and July 2024 (3,7)

12. England's opening opponents at the 2024 ICC Men's T20 World Cup (8)

Answers on page 60

WORD SEARCH

Find the words in the grid. Words can go horizontally, vertically and diagonally in all eight directions.

A	C	P	N	U	W	F	C	Z	H	A	U	F	F	U
E	R	N	R	T	L	A	S	U	Y	L	S	R	P	X
V	X	C	R	Y	L	S	I	N	R	C	G	Q	A	T
V	P	C	H	T	K	E	V	Y	B	R	O	O	K	Z
X	S	J	N	E	X	C	W	W	I	X	A	D	F	A
C	C	E	Z	C	R	O	P	I	H	R	R	N	Q	X
I	M	D	H	Y	P	L	W	J	H	I	W	E	L	B
X	S	D	M	D	G	P	N	N	W	G	D	L	C	K
H	I	J	A	L	C	A	P	J	G	F	I	H	K	Z
V	A	X	L	J	I	D	K	H	O	L	A	X	R	W
D	W	L	E	C	A	L	I	Q	M	R	K	D	M	I
I	Y	L	I	H	U	U	O	H	B	B	D	W	K	V
J	P	G	U	I	P	B	G	Z	S	G	F	A	L	O
T	U	P	R	E	L	T	T	U	B	A	Q	M	N	B
D	C	T	B	L	X	L	S	H	V	H	R	L	W	N

| ALI | BROOK | CURRAN | RASHID |
| ARCHER | BUTTLER | JORDAN | SALT |

2024 T20 WORLD CUP REVIEW

England headed to the 2024 ICC Men's T20 World Cup, which was staged in the West Indies and United States between 1 and 29 June 2024, as reigning champions.

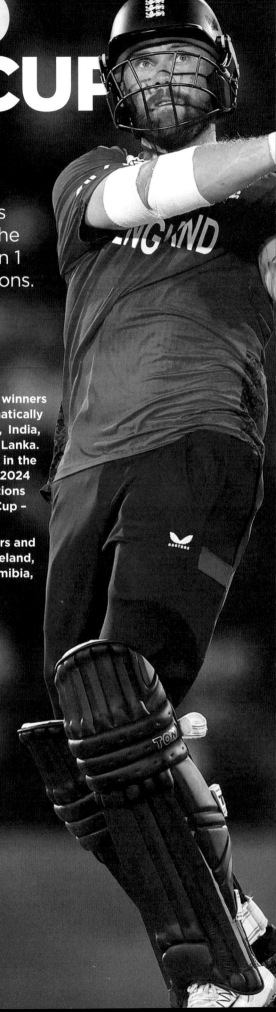

BACKGROUND

By virtue of being one of the top eight teams – indeed, the winners – at the 2022 ICC Men's T20 World Cup, England automatically qualified for the 2024 tournament along with Australia, India, Netherlands, New Zealand, Pakistan, South Africa, and Sri Lanka. Hosts United States and West Indies also took their place in the tournament – which expanded from 16 to 20 teams for the 2024 edition – as did the two highest ranked ICC Men's T20I nations who finished outside the top eight at the previous World Cup – Afghanistan and Bangladesh.

The final eight places were on offer via the Global Qualifiers and the teams to make it to the finals through this path were Ireland, Scotland, Papua New Guinea, Canada, Nepal, Oman, Namibia, and Uganda.

England's 15 player squad was as follows:

17	BEN DUCKETT
18	MOEEN ALI (VICE CAPTAIN)
22	JOFRA ARCHER
23	LIAM LIVINGSTONE
33	MARK WOOD
34	CHRIS JORDAN
38	REECE TOPLEY
51	JONNY BAIRSTOW (WICKETKEEPER)
63	JOS BUTTLER (CAPTAIN, WICKETKEEPER)
79	TOM HARTLEY
58	SAM CURRAN
61	PHIL SALT (WICKETKEEPER)
85	WILL JACKS
88	HARRY BROOK
95	ADIL RASHID

GROUP B

England were placed in Group B of the competition along with Australia, Namibia, Oman, and Scotland. Jos Buttler's side finished second in the group to Australia, joint on five points with third-placed Scotland. England progressed to the Super 8 along with Australia by virtue of a higher run rate with Scotland missing out.

Their results in Group B were as follows:

4 June 2024 Kensington Oval, Bridgetown, West Indies

Umpires: **Nitin Menon** (India) **and Asif Yaqoob** (Pakistan)

SCOTLAND	ENGLAND
90/0 (10 overs)	
Michael Jones 45* (30)	

NO RESULT

8 June 2024 Kensington Oval, Bridgetown, West Indies

Umpires: **Nitin Menon** (India) **and Joel Wilson** (West Indies)

AUSTRALIA	ENGLAND
201/7 (20 overs)	165/6 (20 overs)
David Warner 39 (16)	Jos Buttler 42 (28)
Chris Jordan 2/44 (4 overs)	Pat Cummins 2/23 (4 overs)

AUSTRALIA WON BY 36 RUNS

13 June 2024 Sir Vivian Richards Stadium, North Sound, West Indies

Umpires: **Langton Rusere** (Zimbabwe) **and Asif Yaqoob** (Pakistan)

OMAN	ENGLAND
47 (13.2 overs)	50/2 (3.1 overs)
Shoaib Khan 11 (23)	Jos Buttler 24* (8)
Adil Rashid 4/11 (4 overs)	Kaleemullah 1/10 (1 over)

ENGLAND WON BY 8 WICKETS

15 June 2024 Sir Vivian Richards Stadiym, North Sound, West Indies

Umpires: **Adrian Holdstock** (South Africa) **and Langton Rusere** (Zimbabwe)

ENGLAND	NAMIBIA
122/5 (10 overs)	84/3 (10 overs)
Harry Brook 47* (20)	Michael van Lingen 33 (29)
Ruben Trumpelmann 2/31 (2 overs)	Jofra Archer 1/15 (2 overs)

ENGLAND WON BY 41 RUNS (DLS METHOD)

The final Group B table was:

	TEAM	PLD	W	L	NR	PTS	NRR
1	AUSTRALIA	4	4	0	0	8	2.791
2	ENGLAND	4	2	1	1	5	3.611
3	SCOTLAND	4	2	1	1	5	1.255
4	NAMIBIA	4	1	3	0	2	-2.585
5	OMAN	4	0	4	0	0	-3.062

SUPER 8 – GROUP 2

England's progress in the competition continued as they finished second in their Super 8 group. The victory over the United States (the first T20I meeting of the two nations) was notable as Chris Jordan became the first England player to take a hat-trick in a T20 World Cup.

19 June 2024 Daren Sammy Cricket Ground, Gros Islet, West Indies

Umpires: **Nitin Menon** (India) **and Ahsan Raza** (Pakistan)

WEST INDIES	ENGLAND
180/4 (20 overs)	181/2 (17.3 overs)
Johnson Charles 38 (34)	Phil Salt 87* (47)
Moeen Ali 1/15 (2 overs)	Roston Chase 1/19 (3 overs)

ENGLAND WON BY 8 WICKETS

21 June 2024 Daren Sammy Cricket Ground, Gros Islet, West Indies

Umpires: **Chris Brown** (New Zealand) **and Sharfuddoula** (Bangladesh)

SOUTH AFRICA	ENGLAND
163/6 (20 overs)	156/6 (20 overs)
Quinton de Kock 65 (38)	Harry Brook 53 (37)
Jofra Archer 3/40 (4 overs)	Keshav Maharaj 2/25 (4 overs)

SOUTH AFRICA WON BY 7 RUNS

23 June 2024 Kensington Oval, Bridgetown, West Indies

Umpires: **Chris Gaffaney** (New Zealand) **and Joel Wilson** (West Indies)

UNITED STATES	ENGLAND
115 (18.5 overs)	117/0 (9.4 overs)
Nitish Kumar 30 (24)	Jos Buttler 83* (38)
Chris Jordan 4/10 (2.5 overs)	

ENGLAND WON BY 10 WICKETS

SEMI-FINAL

Despite Chris Jordan taking 3/37 in 3 overs, eventual tournament winners India triumphed against England in the semi-finals with a 68-run victory. India's 7-run win over South Africa in the final saw them join England and West Indies as the ICC Men's T20 World Cup's most successful teams with two trophy triumphs apiece.

27 June 2024 Providence Stadium, Georgetown, West Indies

Umpires: **Chris Gaffaney** (New Zealand) **and Rod Tucker** (Australia)

INDIA	ENGLAND
171/7 (20 overs)	103 (16.4 overs)
Rohit Sharma 57 (39)	**Harry Brook** 25 (19)
Chris Jordan 3/37 (3 overs)	**Kuldeep Yadav** 3/19 (4 overs)

INDIA WON BY 68 RUNS

2025 ICC
WOMEN'S CRICKET
WORLD CUP

At the time of writing, England Women were looking to secure their place at the 2025 ICC Women's Cricket World Cup by virtue of a top-five finish in the 2022–2025 ICC Women's Championship. A total of eight teams will compete at the tournament, including hosts India and reigning champions Australia, who won their seventh title in 2022.

First staged back in 1973, the 2025 ICC Women's Cricket World Cup will be the competition's 13th edition. England staged and then won the first tournament. England's two other World Cup victories to date, in 1993 and 2017, were also achieved on home soil.

The 2025 ICC Women's Cricket World Cup gets underway in September 2025. More information will be available closer to the start of the tournament at www.ecb.co.uk

A Matter of Life & CRICKET!

Guitarist for 86TVs (and formerly of The Maccabees), Felix White is a passionate England cricket fan. Co-host of the cricket-themed podcast Tailenders with England legend James Anderson and radio DJ Greg James since 2017, Felix documented his love of both cricket and music in his 2022 Sunday Times Bestseller and BBC Radio 4 Book of the Week, *It's Always Summer Somewhere: A Matter of Life and Cricket*. Along with Anderson and James, Felix delivered the 2024 MCC Cowdrey Lecture.

Photographs: Shireen Bahmanizad

Tailenders podcast, TBI media for BBC Radio 5 Live

WHERE DOES YOUR INTEREST IN CRICKET STEM FROM?

When I was young, about five or six, it seemed like cricket was always on terrestrial television. It was an omnipresent for me. My parents weren't into cricket, but my grandad was. My parents used to drive me to my grandparents every weekend and he'd have it on.

The positively coincidental thing about that England team of my childhood was that it was so full of wonderful characters, who had their flaws too. As an impressionable youngster, seeing someone like Phil Tufnell on my television for five days, who looked as if he was afraid of the ball and couldn't bat but was still this amazing international cricketer blew my mind. I loved that cricket was a sport that allowed these eccentricities that you simply wouldn't get in other sports.

Over the years, I've done a lot of unpacking of just why cricket has been so important to me.

WHAT ARE YOUR EARLIEST MEMORIES OF AN ENGLAND TEST?

The first Test series I remember watching on the television was the Ashes back in 1993. It felt like a beautiful cinematic set-up in terms of the Australians being the 'bad guys' as they'd be chewing gum. As a kid, they looked like the villains out of Thundercats or something! And there was the England team, the fragile and wary looking 'goodies'.

The first Test I was at was the final Test of the New Zealand series at the Oval in 1999. The defeat in that series infamously saw us go bottom of the world Test rankings. Being at that game cemented my love for the England team. I felt it was the start of a journey which began at the bottom. In a strange way, having that loss and hurt in my early days following England really nailed in the passion I had for the England team.

WHAT HAVE BEEN YOUR HIGHLIGHTS SUPPORTING ENGLAND OVER T HE YEARS?

The journey I have just mentioned culminated for me in winning the Ashes in

45

A Matter of Life & CRICKET!

2005. That was the same year The Maccabees had moved to Brighton and just got a record deal. It's funny how these moments in your life run so intrinsically alongside cricket. That 2005 team was about possibility and denying what had previously been expected of you. I'd have been 20 at the time and that fed into my imagination that the world was for the taking! That team really did speak to me in that sense.

The second Test of that series, especially at Edgbaston, was absolutely incredible... the narrowest Ashes win of all time and all culminating in that incredible feeling of euphoria with the final Test finishing in a draw and us ending that 16-year wait for the Ashes.

AND WHAT A MOMENT IT WAS FOR ENGLAND WINNING THE ICC CRICKET WORLD CUP IN 2019?
I had started doing Tailenders with Jimmy (Anderson) by that point in my life so covering cricket had become part of my professional life then. I was suddenly on the inside. We broadcast before TMS (Test Match Special) came on BBC Radio 5 Live.

Winning that World Cup, and in the circumstances we did, was incredible... beyond words. It's the most emotional I have ever been at a sporting event. I cried my eyes out. I don't think I'll ever cry my eyes out again at cricket because it needed that team never to have won the World Cup before to have the significance that it did.

HAVE YOU FOLLOWED ENGLAND OVERSEAS AT ALL?
I went to The Ashes in 2016. I went to Grenada for the Test in the West Indies more recently. Jimmy's never forgiven me for that one, because he wasn't picked, and I went anyway! I said it was to represent Tailenders, but I obviously just wanted to go!

I went to the 2015 World Cup in Australia. I went to the quarterfinals, semi-finals and final. I obviously hoped I'd be watching England but by the time I got out there, they'd been knocked out. I went to India-Bangladesh and some other matches.

WHO HAVE BEEN YOUR FAVOURITE PLAYERS OVER THE YEARS?
When I was young, it was definitely Phil Tufnell. He was my hero. Having found that association with left-arm spinners, there have been many left-arm spin bowlers I've admired – even non-Englishmen. I think of Daniel Vettori from that series. It didn't seem like he should be an elite sportsperson, but he was. Jack Leach is an obvious one I have to mention.

> **"WINNING THAT WORLD CUP, AND IN THE CIRCUMSTANCES WE DID, WAS INCREDIBLE... BEYOND WORDS."**

I always seem to have a deep fondness for left-arm spinners as they often have a quirk and eccentricity. Just seeing that natural float a left-arm spinner will get on a ball into a right-handed batter, it's different to any other delivery. There's something artistic about what they do that no one else could do.

Continuing on that theme, I'm a huge Sophie Ecclestone fan. Her ability to get the ball up and down and loop like she does is amazing. I love watching her bowl.

AND SURELY JAMES ANDERSON IS ONE OF YOUR FAVOURITE PLAYERS OF ALL-TIME TOO?!
Jimmy's a funny one. Before I met him, I'd seen him so much on television it was almost like he wasn't a real person. Nowadays, I see him as much as anyone in my life, I forget he's 'that Jimmy Anderson'. It's almost like they are two different people.

What has been incredible from spending a lot of time with Jimmy is you see what it must be like to be the parent or partner of a sportsperson. You feel their professional hurt, possibly more than even they do! It certainly added to the intensity of watching England over the last five years, that's for sure!

I ghostwrote Jimmy's book a few years

ago so I can probably tell you more about his career than he could!

WHAT'S YOUR FAVOURITE VENUE TO WATCH AN ENGLAND MATCH?

The Oval is my favourite. It's one of the best grounds in any sport in my opinion. I am a huge Fulham FC supporter and there are parallels between The Oval and Craven Cottage in that you can trace time looking at the various stands. You can sense and feel everything that's gone before. What I also like is it's not too big that it's overwhelming. There's still that sense you can reach out and touch it!

> **"FROM 17 TO MID-30s, MACCABEES WAS MY ENTIRE LIFE. IT'S IMPOSSIBLE TO SUM IT UP."**

TAILENDERS WAS LAUNCHED IN NOVEMBER 2017 AND CONTINUES TO BE RELEASED EVERY WEEK. CAN YOU TELL US A BIT MORE ABOUT YOUR PODCAST JOURNEY?

Tailenders has been a magical part of my life and something I'll always be so grateful for. The Maccabees had just ended back in 2017 and I was in that moment in my life, wondering what was next. It was all I had known. I was 33 but I felt like I didn't know how to do anything else.

Jimmy had come to a few Maccabees gigs, and I knew Greg James liked cricket. Greg dreamed it up and called me and said, 'let's do a show'. We just thought it was going to be a few episodes while Jimmy was out in Australia. At the time, it was a case of 'wow, I'm going to speak to Jimmy Anderson three times'. Seven years later, we're still putting it together every week. It's taken on a complete life of its own.

WHAT WAS IT LIKE PRESENTING THE 2024 MCC COWDREY LECTURE?

The Cowdrey Lecture has obviously been delivered by greats of the game and the thought that the MCC might want us to do it was literally inconceivable. It was a really nice event. The MCC and the Cowdrey family felt if we could bring in that feeling of why we love cricket and

bring that energy, that would work well. We went into a really welcoming environment and there was just a lot of positivity about it.

IN TERMS OF YOUR MUSIC CAREER, HOW DO YOU LOOK BACK ON YOUR TIME WITH THE MACCABEES?

From 17 to mid-30s, Maccabees was my entire life. It's impossible to sum it up. I was in this band with my brothers that got bigger and bigger. All the stuff you hear about bands was true of my experiences. It was amazing. It's lovely hearing younger bands now describing what they are going through, what stage they are at and relating to that.

AND CAN YOU TELL US A BIT MORE ABOUT YOUR CURRENT BAND, 86TVS?

86TVs isn't the only thing in my life like Maccabees was. I've learned that if you grip things too tight, you can squeeze the life out of it. We're all approaching 86TVs with that mindset, focusing on 86TVs but also the other things we do too. When we started out with The Maccabees, we had other jobs and we played together because we enjoyed it. There was no obligation around it. It was music for music's sake. We've captured that with 86TVs. Singing with your brothers is described as 'blood harmony' and it's a very cool thing.

○ Check out 86TVs on Instagram **@86tvsband**

47

MATCH

PAKISTAN WOMEN IN ENGLAND
11-19 MAY 2024 (WT20I SERIES)

Sophie Ecclestone created a major piece of history during the WT20I series whitewash against Pakistan in May 2024. In the second WT20I at the County Ground, Northampton, the slow left-armer's first wicket - caught and bowled off Muneeba Ali – saw her become the leading wicket-taker for England in WT20Is, with 115 wickets. Ecclestone surpassed the previous record held by Katherine Sciver-Brunt as she went on to finish with figures of 3-11 in that match. The series was also notable for Amy Jones playing her 100th WT20I, as she put in a Player of the Match performance in the first WT20I at Edgbaston.

SCORECARD

1st WT20I / 11 May 2024
Edgbaston, Birmingham

Umpires: **Kim Cotton** (New Zealand) and **Sue Redfern** (England)
Player of the Match: **Amy Jones** (England)

ENGLAND ✚	PAKISTAN
163/6 (20 overs)	110 (18.2 overs)
Heather Knight 49 (44)	Sadaf Shamas 35 (24)
Waheeda Akhtar 2/20 (4 overs)	Sarah Glenn 4/12 (4 overs)

ENGLAND WON BY 53 RUNS

ACTION

2nd WT20I / 17 May 2024
County Ground, Northampton

Umpires: **Anna Harris** (England) and **Sue Redfern** (England)
Player of the Match: **Alice Capsey** (England)

ENGLAND	PAKISTAN
144/6 (20 overs)	**79** (15.5 overs)
Nat Sciver-Brunt 31 (21)	Aliya Riaz 19 (17)
Nida Dar 2/33 (4 overs)	Sophie Ecclestone 3/11 (2.5 overs)

ENGLAND WON BY 65 RUNS

3rd WT20I / 19 May 2024
Headingley, Leeds

Umpires: **Kim Cotton** (New Zealand) and **Sue Redfern** (England)
Player of the Match: **Danni Wyatt-Hodge** (England)

ENGLAND	PAKISTAN
176/10 (20 overs)	**142/4** (20 overs)
Danni Wyatt-Hodge 87 (48)	Aliya Riaz 35* (27)
Diana Baig 3/46 (4 overs)	Sophie Ecclestone 1/19 (4 overs)

ENGLAND WON BY 34 RUNS

ENGLAND WON THE SERIES 3-0

49

MATCH

PAKISTAN WOMEN IN ENGLAND
23-29 MAY 2024 (WODI SERIES)

I n addition to becoming England's record wicket-taker in WT20Is, Pakistan's tour of England in May 2024 also saw Sophie Ecclestone become the fastest female cricketer to achieve 100 wickets (in terms of innings - 63) in WODIs. Starting the third WODI against Pakistan on 98 scalps, Ecclestone removed Umm-e-Hani (4) and then reached her 100th WODI wicket as Nashra Sandhu was caught at slip for a duck with consecutive deliveries in the 28th over in the 178-run triumph. She finished that game 3-15, as she also claimed the wicket of Aliya Riaz.

SCORECARD

1st WODI / 23 May 2024
County Ground, Derby

Umpires: **Kim Cotton** (New Zealand) and **Sue Redfern** (England)
Player of the Match: **Sophie Ecclestone** (England)

ENGLAND ✚	🇵🇰 PAKISTAN
243/9 (50 overs)	**206/9** (50 overs)
Alice Capsey 44 (65)	**Muneeba Ali** 34 (60)
Nida Dar 3/56 (10 overs)	**Sophie Ecclestone** 3/26 (10 overs)

ENGLAND WON BY 37 RUNS

ACTION

2nd WODI / 26 May 2024
County Ground, Taunton

Umpires: **Anna Harris** (England) and **Sue Redfern** (England)
Player of the Match: **N/A**

PAKISTAN	ENGLAND
29/0 (6.5 overs)	
Sadaf Shamas 18* (28)	

NO RESULT (MATCH ABANDONED DUE TO RAIN)

3rd WODI / 29 May 2024
County Ground, Chelmsford

Umpires: **Kim Cotton** (New Zealand) and **Jasmine Naeem** (England)
Player of the Match: **Nat Sciver-Brunt** (England)

ENGLAND	PAKISTAN
302/5 (50 overs)	**124** (29.1 overs)
Nat Sciver-Brunt 124* (117)	**Muneeba Ali** 47 (55)
Umm-e-Hani 2/47 (10 overs)	**Sophie Ecclestone** 3/15 (4.1 overs)

ENGLAND WON BY 178 RUNS

ENGLAND WON THE SERIES 2-0

MATCH

PAKISTAN IN ENGLAND
22-30 MAY 2024

In preparation for the 2024 ICC T20 World Cup, Pakistan toured England to play four T20I matches. Sadly, the first and third fixtures - scheduled to be played at Headingley, Leeds and Sophia Gardens, Cardiff – were abandoned due to rain. When the series got underway at Edgbaston 25 May 2024, Jofra Archer made a welcome return to international action, having been sidelined for over a year due to injury. England went on to win the series 2-0.

SCORECARD

1st T20I / 22 May 2024
Headingley, Leeds

Umpires: **Russell Warren** (England) and **Alex Wharf** (England)
Player of the Match: **N/A**

ENGLAND		PAKISTAN

NO PLAY WAS POSSIBLE DUE TO RAIN

SCORECARD

2nd T20I / 25 May 2024
Edgbaston, Birmingham

Umpires: **Mike Burns** (England) and **Martin Saggers** (England)
Player of the Match: **Jos Buttler** (England)

ENGLAND	PAKISTAN
183/7 (20 overs)	**160** (19.2 overs)
Jos Buttler 84 (51)	**Fakhar Zaman** 45 (21)
Shaheen Afridi 3/36 (4 overs)	**Stuart Broad** 4/61 (14.2 overs)

ENGLAND WON BY 23 RUNS

ACTION

3rd T20I / 28 May 2024
Sophia Gardens, Cardiff

Umpires: **Mike Burns** and **Russell Warren** (England)
Player of the Match: **N/A**

ENGLAND 	PAKISTAN

NO PLAY WAS POSSIBLE DUE TO RAIN

4th T20I / 30 May 2024
The Oval, London

Umpires: **Mike Burns** (England) and **Martin Saggers** (England)
Player of the Match: **Adil Rashid** (England)

PAKISTAN 	ENGLAND
157 (19.5 overs)	**158/3** (15.3 overs)
Usman Khan 38 (21)	Phil Salt 45 (25)
Liam Livingstone 2/17 (3 overs)	Haris Rauf 3/38 (3.3 overs)

ENGLAND WON BY 7 WICKETS

ENGLAND WON THE SERIES 2-0

MATCH

NEW ZEALAND WOMEN IN ENGLAND
26 JUNE-3 JULY 2024 (WODI SERIES)

England stepped up their preparations for the 2024 ICC Women's T20 World Cup with an impressive T20I clean sweep against New Zealand. Maia Bouchier hit an impressive 186 runs over the three matches to be named Player of the Series. Her 100* off 88 balls in the 8-wicket victory in the second WODI at New Road was her first WODI century. Lauren Bell was the star of the show in the third WODI as she took her first 5-wicket haul in WODI cricket.

SCORECARD

1st WODI / 26 June 2024
Riverside Ground, Chester-le-Street

Umpires: **Anna Harris** (England) and **Robert White** (England)
Player of the Match: **Charlie Dean** (England)

NEW ZEALAND	ENGLAND
156 (33.3 overs)	**157/1** (21.2 overs)
Brooke Halliday 51 (60)	**Tammy Beaumont** 76* (69)
Charlie Dean 4/38 (9 overs)	**Brooke Halliday** 1/17 (3.2 overs)

ENGLAND WON BY 9 WICKETS

ACTION

2nd WODI / 30 June 2024
New Road, Worcester

Umpires: **Jasmine Naeem** (England) and **Russell Warren** (England)
Player of the Match: **Maia Bouchier** (England)

NEW ZEALAND	ENGLAND
141 (41.5 overs)	142/2 (24.3 overs)
Amelia Kerr 43 (86)	Maia Bouchier 100* (88)
Sophie Ecclestone 5/25 (9 overs)	Brooke Halliday 1/11 (2 overs)

ENGLAND WON BY 8 WICKETS

3rd WODI / 3 July 2024
County Ground, Bristol

Umpires: **Anna Harris** (England) and **Robert White** (England)
Player of the Match: **Lauren Bell** (England)

NEW ZEALAND	ENGLAND
211/8 (42 overs)	212/5 (38.4 overs)
Amelia Kerr 57 (42)	Nat Sciver-Brunt 76* (84)
Lauren Bell 5/37 (9 overs)	Hannah Rowe 2/38 (9 overs)

ENGLAND WON BY 5 WICKETS

ENGLAND WON THE SERIES 3-0

MATCH

NEW ZEALAND WOMEN IN ENGLAND
6-17 JULY 2024 (WT20I SERIES)

After a 3-match victory over New Zealand in the WODI series, England also completed a WT20I whitewash against the visiting Kiwis. Player of the Series Sarah Glenn took eight wickets during the WT20I series as did Sophie Ecceston while Alice Capsey was England's top run scorer with 129 across the series, including 67* in the third WT20I at Canterbury. Amy Jones played her 200th international in the first WT20I – the same match in which Charlie Dean took her 100th international wicket. The second WT20I saw Heather Knight score her 2,000th run in WT20I cricket.

SCORECARD

1st WT20I / 6 July 2024
Utilita Bowl, Southampton

Umpires: **James Middlebrook** (England) and **Sue Redfern** (England)
Player of the Match: **Danni Wyatt-Hodge** (England)

ENGLAND 	NEW ZEALAND
197/3 (20 overs)	**138** (20 overs)
Danni Wyatt-Hodge 76 (51)	Suzie Bates 43 (33)
Lea Tahuhu 2/34 (4 overs)	Sarah Glenn 3/16 (4 overs)

ENGLAND WON BY 59 RUNS

SCORECARD

2nd WT20I / 9 July 2024
County Ground, Hove

Umpires: **Anna Harris** (England) and **James Middlebrook** (England)
Player of the Match: **Charlie Dean** (England)

ENGLAND 	NEW ZEALAND
89/6 (9 overs)	**42/5** (6.4 overs)
Alice Capsey 28 (15)	Brooke Halliday 14 (9)
Lea Tahuhu 2/20 (2 overs)	Charlie Dean 2/3 (1 over)

ENGLAND WON BY 23 RUNS (DLS METHOD)

ACTION

3rd WT20I / 11 July 2024
Spitfire Ground, Canterbury

Umpires: **James Middlebrook** (England) **and Sue Redfern** (England)
Player of the Match: **Alice Capsey** (England)

NEW ZEALAND	ENGLAND
141/8 (20 overs)	**142/4** (19.2 overs)
Sophie Devine 58* (42)	**Alice Capsey** 67* (60)
Sophie Ecclestone 4/25 (4 overs)	**Fran Jonas** 2/23 (4 overs)

ENGLAND WON BY 6 WICKETS

4th WT20I / 13 July 2024
The Oval, London

Umpires: **Anna Harris** (England) and **James Middlebrook** (England)
Player of the Match: **Sarah Glenn** (England)

NEW ZEALAND	ENGLAND
103/8 (20 overs)	**104/3** (11.3 overs)
Izzy Gaze 25 (24)	**Sophia Dunkley** 26 (16)
Sarah Glenn 4/19 (4 overs)	**Eden Carson** 2/11 (2 overs)

ENGLAND WON BY 7 WICKETS

5th WT20I / 17 July 2024
Lord's, London

Umpires: **James Middlebrook** (England) **and Sue Redfern** (England)
Player of the Match: **Heather Knight** (England)

ENGLAND	NEW ZEALAND
197/3 (20 overs)	**135/8** (20 overs)
Heather Knight 46* (31)	**Amelia Kerr** 43 (36)
Fran Jonas 4/22 (4 overs)	**Lauren Bell** 3/21 (4 overs)

ENGLAND WON BY 20 RUNS
ENGLAND WON THE SERIES 5-0

MATCH

WEST INDIES IN ENGLAND
10-30 JULY 2024

Gus Atkinson shone against the West Indies as he became just the twelfth England player to take two five-wicket hauls on a Test debut in the first match of the series at Lord's. He also managed the second-best bowling figures on Test debut by an English cricketer in that match – in which he was one of three debutants along with Jamie Smith and Mikyle Louis. Atkinson took a total of 22 wickets across the three-match series to see him named Player of the Series. Joe Root made 291 runs across during the series, taking his Test run tally past the 12,000-mark in the process. In the third Test at Edgbaston, he scored the fastest-ever half-century for England in a Test match off just 24 balls.

SCORECARD

1st Test / 10-14 July 2024
Lord's, London

Umpires: **Nitin Menon** (India) and **Rod Tucker** (Australia)
Player of the Match: **Gus Atkinson** (England)

WEST INDIES	 ENGLAND
121 (41.4 overs)	371 (90 overs)
Mikyle Louis 27 (58)	Zak Crawley 76 (89)
Gus Atkinson 7/45 (12 overs)	Jayden Seales 4/77 (20 overs)
136 (47 overs)	
Gudakesh Motie 31* (35)	
Gus Atkinson 5/61 (14 overs)	

ENGLAND WON BY AN INNINGS AND 114 RUNS

ACTION

2nd Test / 18-22 July 2024
Trent Bridge, Nottingham

Umpires: **Adrian Holdstock** (South Africa) and **Rod Tucker** (Australia)
Player of the Match: **Ollie Pope** (England)

ENGLAND	WEST INDIES
416 (88.3 overs)	**457** (111.5 overs)
Ollie Pope 121 (167)	**Kavem Hodge** 120 (171)
Alzarri Joseph 3/98 (15.3 overs)	**Chris Woakes** 4/84 (28 overs)
425 (92.2 overs)	**143** (36.1 overs)
Joe Root 122 (178)	**Kraigg Brathwaite** 47 (48)
Jayden Seales 4/97 (22.2 overs)	**Shoaib Bashir** 5/41 (11.1 overs)

ENGLAND WON BY 241 RUNS

---

v PAKISTAN

3rd Test / 26-30 July 2024
Edgbaston, Birmingham

Umpires: **Adrian Holdstock** (South Africa) and **Nitin Menon** (India)
Player of the Match: **Mark Wood** (England)

WEST INDIES	ENGLAND
282 (75.1 overs)	**376** (75.4 overs)
Kraigg Brathwaite 61 (86)	**Jamie Smith** 95 (109)
Gus Atkinson 4/67 (20 overs)	**Alzarri Joseph** 4/122 (17.4 overs)
175 (52 overs)	**87/0** (7.2 overs)
Mikyle Louis 57 (95)	**Ben Stokes** 57* (28)
Mark Wood 5/40 (14 overs)	

ENGLAND WON BY 10 WICKETS
ENGLAND WON THE SERIES 3-0

ANSWERS

CROSS*WORD*

Page 38

WORD*SEARCH*

Page 39

A	C	P	N	U	W	F	C	Z	H	A	U	F	F	U
E	R	N	R	T	L	A	S	U	Y	L	S	R	P	X
V	X	C	R	Y	L	S	I	N	R	C	G	Q	A	T
V	P	C	H	T	K	E	V	Y	B	R	O	O	K	Z
X	S	J	N	E	X	C	W	W	I	X	A	D	F	A
C	C	E	Z	C	R	O	P	I	H	R	R	N	Q	X
I	M	D	H	Y	P	L	W	J	H	I	W	E	L	B
X	S	D	M	D	G	P	N	N	W	G	D	L	C	K
H	I	J	A	L	C	A	P	J	G	F	I	H	K	Z
V	A	X	L	J	I	D	K	H	O	L	A	X	R	W
D	W	L	E	C	A	L	I	Q	M	R	K	D	M	I
I	Y	L	I	H	U	U	O	H	B	B	D	W	K	V
J	P	G	U	I	P	B	G	Z	S	G	F	A	L	O
T	U	P	R	E	L	T	T	U	B	A	Q	M	N	B
D	C	T	B	L	X	L	S	H	V	H	R	L	W	N